ONE PART HONOR

ONE PART HONOR

*Stories and Faces of Chicago's
Olive Branch*

Photos by Sharon Smith and Wally Wright
Text by Jack Dierks • Foreword by Richard M. Daley

**CHICAGO
REVIEW
PRESS**

Library of Congress Cataloging-in-Publication Data

Smith, Sharon.
    One part honor: stories and faces of Chicago's Olive Branch
/ photos by Sharon Smith and Wally Wright: text by Jack Dierks.
—1st ed.
        p. cm.
    Includes bibliographical references.
    ISBN 1-55652-199-5 (pbk.) : $16.95
        1. Homeless persons—Illinois—Chicago—Portraits.   2. Olive
Branch Mission—History.—I. Wright, Wally.—II. Dierks, Jack.
III. Title.
HV4506.C5S63 1993
362.5'09773'11—dc20   93-24032
                                                           CIP

First Edition
Published by Chicago Review Press, Incorporated
814 N. Franklin Street, Chicago, Illinois 60610

ISBN 1-55652-199-5
Printed in the United States of America

5 4 3 2 1

If one part suffers, every part suffers with it:
if one part is honored, every part rejoices with it.

(1 Cor. 12:26)

This project is partially supported by a grant from the City of Chicago Department of Cultural Affairs and the Illinois Arts Council Access Program.

| Contents

| *Foreword*

I've visited the Olive Branch Mission often. I always come away impressed by the dedication of its staff to serving the emergency needs of men, women, and children, and by their efficient management of resources to help as many as possible move from homelessness to independent living.

This book deepens my appreciation for the needs of Olive Branch visitors and the skills of those who serve them. Here, in these outstanding photographs, "the homeless" have faces: there's Charles, solemn, bespectacled, thoughtful; Clifford, hopeful, his eyebrows raised, about to get off the streets and into an apartment; George, an elderly Korean War veteran; a smiling Ernestine, hand at her throat as if she were about to share a confidence; newlyweds Staci and Steve; and many, many more. Enjoy the artistry of photographers Sharon Smith and Wally Wright and the humanity of these Chicagoans who agreed to sit for them. Make eye contact with their faces. Understand that they're our neighbors. Resolve, with me, to renew your commitment to make life in Chicago better for them and for others in need.

Richard M. Daley
Mayor of Chicago

| Preface

The Olive Branch buildings at night
(Photo by Robert McKenrick)

This book has sprung from a desire to add the stories of the Olive Branch Mission founders to Chicago's impressive history of social pioneers, as well as our wish to document life at the mission today. The vision, commitment, and enthusiasm of our volunteers working alongside of the homeless people of Chicago made it happen.

Chicago's history includes tales of titans who established industries and built monuments and of pioneers who served our most severe human needs. The City of Big Shoulders is midway between the City of Angels and the Big Apple in terms of geography, and light-years away from them in terms of spirit. Chicagoans have always understood that those who struggle constitute as much of our gritty history as those who triumph, and that the stories of those who treat its wounded are as significant as those who capture its glory.

Yet the two brave women who founded and nurtured the Olive Branch Mission, Rachael Bradley and Mary Everhart, are known only to the few of us who have read their spellbinding accounts in the century-old newspapers in our offices. Chicago's social history records the considerable accomplishments of such humanitarians as Jane Addams, who founded Hull House; Graham Taylor, "the conscience of Chicago," who founded the Chicago School of Civics and Philanthropy and the Chicago Commons Settlement House; and William Stead, whose scathing book *If Christ Came to Chicago* named leading citizens growing rich from bordellos, politicians who bought elections, even Mayor Harrison, who made lucrative deals with gambling interests when tens of thousands of homeless people tramped the streets. They were more visible than the Olive Branch women, better connected, and well documented: all of them wrote books.

Predating Hull House by thirteen years, the Olive Branch founders went about their work quietly, eventually recording their pleas and experiences only in the newspaper they sent to friends and patrons. Here they advertised for help, asking for a worker who could be, like themselves, "careless of glory":

> Wanted—a worker who's careless of glory,
> Where millions are dying in shame and in sin;
> Oh, where are the reapers? The harvest is waiting—
> Who'll bind up the sheaves and gather them in?

Mary Everhart's thirty-five years at the Olive Branch Mission ended with her death in 1928, but her vision persists. Her vision of educating youth for urban ministry evolved into our Wesleyan Urban Coalition, which has thirteen participating colleges. Mary Everhart also started our newspaper which—as far as we know—is second only to the *Tribune* as Chicago's oldest continuously running paper. Now housed at the Chicago Historical Society, these papers provide a vital history, and they were instrumental in defining the needs of the mission throughout the Midwest. We still get countless checks from elderly people who write that they worked in church kitchens as youngsters in Michigan, Indiana, and Wisconsin to send food to the mission. They never forgot Mary, who had visited their summer church camps to sell twenty-five-cent subscriptions. Today, the paper goes to over 40,000 donors from all over the United States and eight countries.

We wanted to tell of these brave and innovative women, and we also wanted to show life at the Olive Branch Mission today. These wishes came together in 1989 when we were looking for a way to celebrate our 115th anniversary the next year. A public relations volunteer came up with the idea for a photo exhibit, which was the farthest thing from our minds. She enlisted two of America's finest photographers, Sharon Smith and Wally Wright, who said they would spend a year documenting life at the Olive Branch Mission, without charge.

I was stunned that this busy husband-and-wife team would volunteer to spend an entire year with us, while continuing their full-time careers. Little did any of us know it would turn out to be three years!

Before they started to shoot, they came just to observe, to get acquainted, and to listen. We were short-staffed and overcrowded. Our usual mealtime number of 150 had mushroomed to 350 or 400. We had to expand to three meals a day, rather than two on weekdays and one on weekends. By the time Sharon and Wally finished their shooting, we were open twenty-four hours a day, and it was becoming increasingly difficult to find a place for them to set up their equipment. They remained committed, flexible, and always eager to listen to people in ways I no longer had time for.

When I first saw their photos, I was amazed at how they had come into what must have seemed like bedlam and captured such dignity and beauty. I am perhaps most grateful to them for affirming the dream we have always had of making the Olive Branch Mission a place where people could get back in touch with their humanity, not just review their losses.

I had anticipated that many of our guests would choose not to participate in the photo project. I was wrong. Sharon and Wally talked to them about doing something for the mission, and many wanted to give something back to us. Increasingly, they became friends, trusted the photographers, and admired their work. Usually many were waiting in line to be photographed whenever ·Sharon and Wally set up.

In 1990, the *Chicago Tribune* ran nine of the photographs prior to the anniversary exhibit. Businesses and individuals came together to help: typography, flowers, exhibit panels and lighting, refreshments, photo processing and matting, printing, and all of the labor to set up were donated.

Good things continued: a design firm used some of the photos to make Christmas cards for themselves and for us; people called to volunteer in every capacity; institutions requested the exhibit and it has been shown at ten locations; attendees from city government, who had formerly come only to inspect our facilities, gained a new perspective on our work and now frequently turn to us to provide new programs; Sharon and Wally got a grant to continue their work; and Southern Illinois University Press expressed an interest in doing this book.

Sharon and Wally continued to expand their vision, and exhibited newer work in 1991. Jack Dierks offered to write the history, and the book was completed.

Now you, the reader, are a participant in our story. When you look at these photos, you'll see each is unique, but I hope that you'll also discover that they are more like you than they are different from you. Perhaps you will be able to tell that the subjects were concerned about how they would look in front of the camera, how they appear to you. Be aware that hardship hasn't destroyed them: they survive and have hopes and dreams, just as you and I do. I hope you will see that they haven't given up on themselves, and that you won't give up on them either.

Where misconceptions exist about the age, race, and sex of homeless people, or about their needs, I hope they will be dispelled. Perhaps their stories will refute a notion that they could get themselves off of the street unassisted if they wanted to. It is easier for us to harden our hearts if we believe that many homeless people choose to be addicts, rather than learning that addictions are often the last manifestation of a life of tragedy.

I hope this book will lead you to a new sensitivity about the need for services to the homeless, and about how dependent agencies such as the Olive Branch are on understanding neighbors and accepting communities. I hope that you will volunteer at a homeless shelter. If you don't think you have a useful ability, give the staff the opportunity to explain the many ways that volunteers have blessed them. I think you'll find that you also are blessed by your service.

Larry Davis
Executive Director, 1986–1992
Olive Branch Mission

Acknowledgments
Thank you:

To the Olive Branch guests, the subjects of this book, for their willingness to be photographed and to share their lives with us.

To Sharon Smith and Wally Wright, whose artistry speaks for itself on these pages, and whose enthusiasm and vision have blessed all who have been graced by it.

To Larry Davis, the Olive Branch director during the years this work was done, for providing the opportunity to participate and for a steady example of service the rest of us aspire to in our finer moments.

To Jack Dierks, for researching, interviewing, and writing the exciting story of the pioneer Olive Branch women, so that they can take their place in the social history of Chicago and this country.

To Carol DeChant and Kelly Hughes, who coordinated it all from concept to finished book publicity.

To Jan Cullin, who took life story notes at the shoots, many times into the night and again at dawn the next morning; Alan Youngren, who always made shooting space available in some corner of the teeming mission; Gamma Photo Labs, for exquisite prints, and especially Gerald and Stacey, for their trust and help; Harry Anastopoulos of Telusys, Inc. for typesetting; Dick DeBacher for agreeing that this was an important book and guiding its early development; and the City of Chicago and the State of Illinois for a grant to take the shooting into a second year.

To Linda Matthews for her gracious acceptance of this book and guidance of it through publication, and Chicago Review Press for benefiting the work of the Olive Branch by publishing it, and to Jerry Stroud and the Chicago Review Press/Independent Publishers Group sales representatives, who are placing it into America's bookstores, libraries, and museums.

To all the others in that happy band of volunteers—Olive Branch guests, staff, and friends—who shared the once-in-a-lifetime adventure of making this book happen.

To all who read this book. Please keep in touch so I can send you our newsletter.

John Carter Adams, Executive Director
Olive Branch Mission
1047 West Madison Street
Chicago, Illinois 60607

1 *Chicago in the Exposition Year*

No one who was there that day doubted that May 1, 1893, was a culminating triumph for Chicago. Of course, visitors to the World's Columbian Exposition fairgrounds had to sit through some high-toned oratory by Grover Cleveland, but that was soon over. With all.eyes on the podium, and the band nearby ready to break into "Hail, Columbia," the golden telegraph key was handed to him. It took just a single press of the presidential finger to switch on the power in the network of tunnels underneath architect Daniel Burnham's 686-acre spread of neoclassical buildings and thoroughfares, starting up the gas engines, the turbines and dynamos, the textile and meat-packing apparatus in the Machinery Hall; the ponderous gears that operated George Washington Ferris' 265-foot "observation wheel," the half-mile-long moving sidewalk, the circuits that lit up the 74 galleries of sculpture and paintings in the Fine Arts Building and the 6,000 carbon arc and the 120,000 incandescent lamps—more light bulbs than the whole city of Chicago had—which, if it did nothing else, left no doubt in anyone's mind that Mr. Edison's invention was here to stay.

The same could certainly be said for Chicago, as well, and all this gala couldn't have been more fitting. It was time for the city to shrug off any remaining vestiges of those terrible three days twenty-two years before when the fabled O'Leary cow down on DeKoven Street started the blaze that had reduced the town's heart, if not its spirit, to ashes.

The rise from the rubble of 1871 had been swift and impressive. The metropolis now boasted a population of nearly 1.5 million, all drawn to the city that one English newspaper correspondent called the "concentrated essence of Americanism." Chicago was now not only the second most important urban area in the United States, but the fourth largest in the world. The sheer activity level was overwhelming. Carl Sandburg, an eighteen-year-old from Galesburg, Illinois, visited the area for the first time about then, and "walked miles and never got tired of the roar of the street, the trolley cars, the teamsters, the drays, buggies, surreys, and phaetons; the delivery wagons high with boxes, the brewery wagons piled with barrels, the one-horse and two-horse hacks, sometimes a buckboard with a coachman in livery..."

All this bustle was fueled by money, and it seemed to be visible everywhere. The Fields, the McCormicks, the Swifts, and the Armours built impressive mansions, primarily in the Prairie Avenue district, which became known as the "street of the sifted few." Others developed land on "millionaire's row" on South Michigan Avenue. Potter Palmer shelled out hard cash for sand dunes and stagnant frog ponds on the North Side's neglected lake front, filled in the site, and in 1885 took possession of the finest house in Chicago, a turreted, balconied, minareted, porte-cochered granite castle, from which, at her base of operations in either the French drawing room, or the Greek or Japanese parlors, or the Spanish music room, or her Louis XVI bedroom, or perhaps from the sunken Turkish pool adjoining it, his wife Bertha reigned over the town's society. New York's Fifth Avenue had nothing on the Palmers. That was Chicago, Gem of the Prairie, in the Exposition year.

A few blocks to the west, probably closer than was comfortable for the first families of Prairie Avenue, was an area of dilapidated frame houses that were mere remnants of respectable workers' homes that had long since fallen into ruin. Now roofs gaped, walls sagged crazily, and vacant windows stared. Saloons had sprung up everywhere on the nearby streets.

Two women—one middle-aged, one younger—climbed the back stairs of a particularly ramshackle house in the winter of the Exposition year, picking their way carefully over ice, ashes, and every kind of filth. Someone had told them about the children there, and although they didn't know what they would find upstairs, they were used to sights of all kinds. They were from the

Olive Branch Mission, not far away on Des Plaines Street, and when they weren't conducting religious services in the mission building or on the corner nearby, they spent every day visiting places just such as this, or the saloons themselves, or anywhere they felt they might be of help.

The women found four children in the unheated attic room. One was a little girl whimpering in bed under a ragged blanket. She had burned her leg badly from the knee to the foot, and nothing had been done to treat it, except for the application of some ink, considered a rough home remedy. It had done no good at all. The children's mother had been dead for a year; their father made a little money sharpening scissors on the streets. He was out there now. A hoarse, wheezy cough from a corner of the room revealed a hollow-eyed, two-year-old boy with a bad case of the croup. He had been given kerosene internally, and more had been smeared about his neck in such quantities that it had eaten a raw, angry sore all the way around.

The women shivered in the cold. Was there any food in the house? The oldest girl left the room and returned a moment later with a pot. In it were a dozen chicken heads that had been taken from a butcher's garbage can, and would be boiled for dinner with a few strands of macaroni. She was pleased with her find. The visitors got the impression that it was more than the children were used to. In another corner of the room was a big pile of cigar butts. The fourth child, a little boy, told one of the women that he picked them up out of the gutters and sold them for bread. He was quite proud of himself. He almost had enough for a loaf.

The two missionaries left and began searching from house to house, all down the block for someone who would at least bring in a clean cloth and bind up the girl's leg. They knocked on a lot of doors before they found a neighbor woman who agreed to stop by.

The next day they returned with a blanket, a few potatoes, some beans and apples, and a small sack of coal from the stocks that had been contributed to the mission. The day was colder. Much colder. And the woman who had promised to tend to the burned girl had never come at all.

This, too, was life in Chicago in the year of the fair.

The Need for Reform

See them reeling down the street
Bloated faces, stagg'ring feet,
Hair unkept and clothes awry,
Horror of the passer-by,
Are the fruits of Rum!

—*The Olive Branch* newspaper

Front page of *The Olive Branch* newspaper from 1902

A few, like Theodore Dreiser, saw and were able to appreciate both the heights and the depths. As a cub reporter, he covered fires, muggings, and "smash-and-grab" cases for the *Chicago Globe*, while absorbing material for the novels he would one day write. He called Chicago "a very bard of a city...singing of high deeds and high hopes, its heavy brogans buried deep in the mire of circumstance."

The Fourth Estate knew that Mayor Carter Harrison had a notoriously hands-off administration. Throughout his five terms, Harrison believed that prostitution, gambling, and their attendant vices were too ingrained in society for the law to do away with them. So they flourished. Just a few blocks from the fashionable near South Side lakefront was a notorious district known as the Levee, where alleys and dives were alive with harlots, addicts, sneak thieves, and strong-arm gangs. Hundreds of pimps organized into the Cadet's Protective Association, part of a slavery system that maintained stockades, "breaking in" dens, and classes in which young girls were forced into various perversions.

Olive Branch workers found the victims: young women tricked into slavery through mock marriages; girls of every race and color, no longer useful and dying of consumption or other diseases; an eleven-year-old who was sold to a man by her own mother.

The Levee had twenty-five-cent brothels as bad as anything in the nation, and it had the Everleigh Club, a fifty-room bordello mansion run by sisters Ada and Minna, who employed three separate orchestras to entertain customers. The Olive Branch workers were horrified that women would be a party to visiting such misery on young girls. Reporting to the State's Attorney that a French girl had been lured into slavery, a mission worker wrote, "How it adds fuel to the flame of resentment already kindled in our innermost souls to know that the house in which this fifteen-year-old girl was held is only a few doors from the mission home, and that the woman who is said to be carrying it on has a home in Glencoe, Illinois, where she is known by another name than the one by which she was indicted."

The Vice Commission estimated that girls were used up in a big time parlor in five years. Because of this limited life in what the vice lords referred to as "stock," they recruited victims continually. Supplying the large demand for new girls was the well-paying trade of the many procurers, who did their business not only in Chicago, but in large cities across America.

Kidnapping was a common method of recruitment, the Olive Branch workers knew. Their newspaper tells of a young victim named Pearl:

> In September of the World's Fair year, she, then being only seventeen years, came into the city from her home to take the train for LaGrange, where she was employed as an artist. She concluded to

take a streetcar ride to pass away the few hours before her train. Presently a fascinating young woman took her seat by Pearl's side. Her social chat and kind manners soon won Pearl's confidence. . . .

In a burst of enthusiasm the young woman said, "Oh! if you will just stop at my home for a few moments, we will take a car and go to the park, and then I will accompany you to the train!"

Pearl thought that she was fortunate in finding such a pleasant companion and readily accepted the kindly invitation. They entered an elegantly furnished mansion, the door closed behind them, and Pearl found herself a prisoner. After five months of enforced prostitution, Pearl escaped one night when all of the inmates were intoxicated. The women's hearts went out to this girl, obviously from a good background. Why hadn't she gone home? Her mother must be frantic. "With a look of despair which no tongue or pen could describe," Pearl told them that she had contracted a disease during her slavery. Taking her stricken body home in that era would have brought shame on her family. She preferred that they mourn her for dead than know all she had been forced to do.

"God pity and save the victims of such injustice and cruelty," the report concluded.

Many pre-Prohibition Americans believed that drink was one of the most important causes, if not the sole cause, of poverty, indecency, and despair. Olive Branch Mission workers saw much to substantiate this theory. Their newspaper stories offered evidence: "good and virtuous women who link their lives to men who...drink (and then) desert their families, leaving them destitute," and child victims who sorrowed and outraged them. They wrote of Tommy, dying of wounds inflicted by his father, and saying, "I'm glad I'm going to die. I'm too weak to help mother now. In Heaven the angels ain't going to call me a drunkard's child and make fun of my clothes." And of a ten-year-old boy whose feet were crushed by a runaway horse-drawn carriage. When he was told that his legs had been amputated, he worried about who would take care of his drunken father.

In the 1890s, there were nearly seven thousand saloons—one for every two hundred citizens—to serve a Chicago whose residents put away three million barrels of beer annually. By the turn of the century, *The Olive Branch* reported nine thousand saloons and pool rooms in Chicago, with 312 prostitution dens in one ward alone. Its editor decried that there were by comparison so few churches, and these, "mostly clustered in wealthier regions" of the city.

It was on the lowest economic level of society that alcohol abuse was most visible. The convergence of railway lines in Chicago brought more than thirty thousand homeless men to the streets each year during the 1890s, a number that was swelled by seasonal agricultural unemployment. Any national economic slowdown increased the number: during a depression that followed the panic of 1893, as many as seventy-five thousand derelicts filled every type of free sleeping space. They had become the city's most noticeable population segment.

In the summer they filled the parks and alleys and spaces under elevated tracks. "Hobo jungles" were a common sight along any railway line, and there was a large camp at the mouth of the Chicago River. Winter tested them more severely, and the winter of 1893–94 was the harshest in Chicago history. Homeless people died of cold and hunger only a few blocks west of the city's grand lakefront mansions and magnificent World's Fair buildings. As many as two thousand people a night bedded down in the corridors of City Hall. *The Olive Branch* articles told of ministering to drifters who had lost their limbs jumping to board trains, twelve-year-olds who rode stock car trains across the country, a rheumatic woman who had to sleep in a police station her first night out of the hospital. They were from all over the city and all over the world: "a poor Swede with a broken back," "a German woman abandoned with her children," "a Norwegian dying from consumption."

Most drifters satisfied themselves with boiled eggs and cheese and crackers at one of the local saloon's free lunch counters. Chroniclers of those times have called them a literal lifesaver: one estimated that they kept sixty thousand people from starvation every year. The Olive Branch women disagreed strongly, noting that their real purpose was to stimulate the appetite for drink. "The free lunches given out at saloons are very expensive to the one who goes in, costing him four or five dollars in one night for drinks for himself and others," they wrote. They reminded readers of the ultimate cost: over sixty thousand alcoholics died annually in the United States.

It was all part of the system in Chicago. *The Olive Branch* editors lamented that "this year, as in many previous, two saloon keepers in this ward ran for aldermen." But their greater outrage was for the good people who remained uninvolved. "We do not see how any Christian dare avoid the duties of citizenship. Only a moral coward will dare nurse and pamper his refined feelings and skulk away amidst kindred spirits while this terrible monster sweeps our best, our dearest into the very mouth of the pit. As we gaze into these awful hellholes that you 'amen' at the ballot box…our very souls cry out in indignation." The Olive Branch women, who ministered to those who suffered alcohol's terrible consequences, had no use for refined Christian men who declared that "you cannot keep the grace of God in your heart and have anything to do with politics." Such Christianity was not suitable for Chicago.

An Enthusiasm for Service

Be not simply good, but be good for something.
—The Olive Branch newspaper, 1896

The Olive Branch founder Rachael Bradley

Chicago itself was a phenomenon that grew out of the aftermath of the Civil War, that conflagration that changed so much in American life. The war had devastated the South and, by speeding up the process of industrialization and urbanization of recently arrived immigrant groups in the North, had created massive problems of crowding and deprivation in cities like Chicago.

War work acquainted many Americans with the necessity of aiding those who suffered. For many women, war relief work was an emancipating experience. It made some rueful, after the fighting had ended, to return once again to the management of households. Indeed, that was impossible for the many whose husbands, or the young men who might have married them, had been casualties. That generation of women carried forward into postwar America the enthusiasm for service that had been awakened between 1861 and 1865. They were the foremothers and the teachers of those who came after, who were to make the Progressive Era famous for selfless women who devoted their lives to aiding the unfortunate.

Mary Everhart was one of these, although she would never describe herself in such glorified terms. She was born on a farm near Lickingville, Pennsylvania, in February 1853, the granddaughter of a Scottish Methodist preacher. She had grown up with a strong determination to plot her own course in life, a quality that was immediately tested in a conflict with her father, who felt that her ambition to teach was encroaching on man's work. His approval was won grudgingly, but she settled into the work with enthusiasm, and taught for twenty years before moving to Chicago in 1890 to take a position in the Industrial Home for Children. The superintendent there thought he detected in her a potential for mission work, and suggested she help out at Mrs. Rachael Bradley's center on Wells Street.

Mrs. Bradley had started up a Saturday sewing class for the neighborhood poor back in 1876 in the Free Methodist Church on Morgan Street. She felt that the class didn't provide enough opportunity to minister to the needy, so she decided to add Bible teaching to the activities and located an old hall on Wells Street for that purpose. In the large single room that served as both working and living quarters, she preached the love of God in the midst of Chicago's slums for sixteen years.

In 1891, the mission moved to Des Plaines Street, just three blocks south of Haymarket Square, where eleven had been killed and over a hundred wounded during an anarchists' labor demonstration on May 4, 1886. The mission's name was changed to the Olive Branch Mission, not long after Mary Everhart came to help the older woman out on Christmas, the busiest day of the calendar.

Mary found the once tall and regal Mrs. Bradley in terrible circumstances.

"She was lodged by a stranger on the third floor of a rooming house, sick, oh, so sick! The few pennies I carried to her from friends were all she had to supply her with food and medicine," her protégé later wrote. "Although it meant death by inches, with her iron will and her tender loving heart, she pushed on the battle" to keep the mission going.

A year and a half after the helper came, Mrs. Bradley sold all the mission equipment to Mary with the stipulation that, if she recovered, she would buy it back. She did not. On August 30, 1893, with the World's Fair in full swing, Mary Everhart became the new owner and superinten-

Mary Everhart, superintendent of the Olive Branch from 1893 to 1928

dent, reporting sadly that "now others not so capable are taking on the work of the Olive Branch."

At this time, institutions like the Olive Branch Mission did not have a long history. In the latter half of the nineteenth century, the American attitude toward poverty was an amalgam of two conflicting views: Calvinism taught that poverty was a manifestation of God's will, perhaps not wholly comprehensible, but a blessing of sorts, for it inspired the rich to acts of personal charity and led the poor onto paths of patience and gratitude. Opposed to this, American experience suggested that poverty was unnecessary.

Most nineteenth-century Americans combined these views into the following belief: Poverty ought to be unnecessary in the United States, but people's varying abilities and virtues made poverty impossible to do away with. "For the poor always ye have with you." (John 12:8) This creed attributes destitution to man rather than God. The favored were obligated to aid the unfortunate, but popular thinking emphasized the responsibility of each individual to look out for his own interests, promoting a see-no-evil attitude.

The belief that personal failings caused poverty retained a popular following long after the disappearance of the economic circumstances that seemed to give it validity. It was particularly difficult for nineteenth-century Americans to accept that, in a complex economy, individuals were no longer the independent entities they once seemed to be, that an impersonal element had begun to operate in the economic area, and that it was increasingly apparent that people suffered as often from the venality and blunders of others as from their own shortcomings.

Mary Everhart changed her views on these matters during her work with prostitutes. "I once believed that almost everyone of this class had deliberately chosen this life, but I now know that at least 75 percent were unwilling victims…snared, trapped, bought, and sold" or desperate to provide for their children.

"It is an alarming fact that many of our fallen sisters have become such through the cruel hand of oppression and the lack of timely aid and sympathy. Many of the girls who work in our factories and are employed as clerks in our stores…find their income inadequate." They become tempted "to sell their virtue to supply the lack, never dreaming of becoming public prostitutes," Mary wrote, dismayed that it usually became their fate. A number of Protestant clergy began to devote attention to this emerging awareness, and to the problems arising from rapid industrial urban growth. The sermons that grew out of their efforts were designed to make their middle-class congregations realize their responsibility for justice and see that the conditions under which men and women labored, and the circumstances in which they spent their lives, posed moral questions requiring every Christian's attention.

Mary Everhart also posed these questions—and answered them—in *The Olive Branch* newspaper, which she started in 1894:

Who is responsible (for a woman prostituting herself to support her five children)?

If the Christian world were more like Him who went about the visiting of the afflicted, relieving the oppressed, and binding up broken hearts, there would be fewer such testimonies as [this woman's]. We make no excuses for sin, but insomuch as we fold our arms and turn a deaf ear to those crying for help, just ready to plunge headlong into ruin and utter despair, we are responsible for their sin.

Is it enough to gather the children of Christian and moral parents into our churches and teach them the truths of Christianity?

No!

For the most part, though, Mary and her colleagues didn't concern themselves with the day's social and theological theories. There was work to be done, and their focus was on how best to serve the incredible needs in their midst. Their mission was simple and practical, as was their faith: "A religion that feeds the bodies as well as the souls of men, where workers go into the slums, visit the needy sick, scrub their floors, bathe their bodies, give them food, watch with them at night, clothe them, and, besides pray with them and get them saved, must commend itself to all sincere lovers of the human race."

Their lives were never simple. The neighborhood where Mary Everhart took it upon herself to work was wretched. At one time there were thirteen saloons in the block where the mission was located, and 337 within three-quarters of a mile. Every other house on the block was a brothel. The police warned Mary that the alley adjacent to the mission was the most dangerous in the city after dark. Their building was a ramshackle wreck, always in danger of being condemned by the Health Department. It was infested with rats, which customarily crawled into the walls to die. Mission workers burned apple parings to try and get rid of the odor, unsuccessfully.

In spite of the grim surroundings—or, in another sense, because of them—Mary Everhart's work was pressing, and her typical week was hectic. There were services at the Olive Branch Mission every evening. Workers and converts met at the mission at 7 P.M. for prayer, gathering in the one large room that held two hundred people. Singing was a big part of the service, with Mary and another one of the sisters—both of whom had good voices—leading the congregation. An appointed leader addressed the audience. Then converts told their stories of redemption, and there was an altar service. Because the congregations were made up largely of alcoholics, precautions had to be taken: those who went to the altar took their hats and other belongings; otherwise, they might be stolen while they prayed.

Then a meal was served on long tables. At some time during the evening, if the weather permitted, they would all walk half a block to the corner of Madison and Des Plaines streets for an open-air meeting.

Each Wednesday afternoon the workers visited the Cook County Hospital. They also frequently visited the state penitentiary in Joliet, sometimes getting prisoners released in their custody. On Sunday mornings, they visited inmates at the neighborhood police station. On the way home they would hold a service in the lodging house where the mission workers lived, and after the noon meal, there would be a Sunday school for both children and adults. In addition, there were meetings to provide ongoing spiritual help and to encourage attendees towards a moral life. There were all-day services on Christmas and Thanksgiving and often on other holidays as well. For years the workers ran a live-in rescue home for abandoned and orphaned children, located three blocks from the mission.

There were also continual rounds of visitation in homes, lodging houses, and saloons, which were considered important targets of their ministry. (A local dive offered ten-dollar rewards to anyone who would draw a mission convert back into drinking.) Usually two of the women walked in together for mutual protection. Mary Everhart once stopped by forty-five saloons in one day, and for a time she conducted a weekly gospel service in one of the worst of them, with the owner's permission. The police warned her that someday she would be murdered in a saloon for the "ten-cent collection" boxes she always carried. It didn't happen, although she was once threatened by a saloon owner who felt she was ruining his business. Another time, she incurred deep facial cuts and bruises after being chased and run down by cyclists.

Back at the mission there was food and donated clothing to tally and distribute, and the monthly newspaper to edit and mail. The newspaper pleaded for twenty-five cents a year for subscriptions: "I think many times it would be much easier to pay twenty-five cents to read about this work in the slums and dens in the city than to do the work. Which will you do? Don't say 'neither.'"

The Olive Branch became a valuable documentation of ministering to Chicago's indigent. By tireless selling of newspaper subscriptions and her summertime church camp visits, Mary extended awareness and participation in the Olive Branch work all over the Midwest, and eventually throughout the United States.

There were also great piles of letters to answer, meals to cook and serve, laundry to wash, and the endless task of keeping the household clean in an area blackened by the smoke of coal fires. And the purely mundane:

> Dear readers:
> When you pluck a fowl, please singe it too. You see, when they come to us frozen, it is almost impossible to singe them.
> We are having trouble with moths in this intense August heat in our crowded quarters, so please save all clothing donations until October.
> We have to pay twenty-four cents a pound for butter. Please can someone send us a five-quart pail?

Most of her challenges were more serious, like the time she and a coworker, searching for a young girl in need, found themselves in a basement opium dive in a dark, filthy alley: "We were obliged to go in or be defeated in our purpose. The only light that could be seen in that dungeon was from tapers lighted for opium smoking. Two beds held both men and women gathered to smoke freely. Such a burden came upon us for the souls of these poor girls in the jaws of hell that we burst into tears, and between sobs and cries told them …how our loving Savior could bring them up out of this horrible pit."

As traumatic as this first visit was for the missionaries, they returned several times, "hoping to reach those girls so hardened, so stubborn, so skeptical."

Eventually, the police "began pulling the opium joints," Mary wrote, "so their door became closed to us and we lost sight of these girls forever."

It was all in a day's work for Mary, who let neither the general viciousness of the neighborhood or her own bad health deter her. She felt that God was employing her for his own purposes, and she would not falter. "He can use a worm to thresh a mountain," she was fond of saying.

Mary became ill in 1895, then two years later she and Jennie Clark and Viletta Dalrymple were stricken with "la grippe." Viletta was sent away to recover from a diseased lung; a year later Jennie, still ill, was sent to California to recover; and Mary struggled on.

During these months of sickness, Mary's newspaper pieces sometimes revealed discouragement, even desperation: "We need helpers. I have toiled almost night and day for years, but I cannot toil on as I have done, and we cannot have any more help unless we have more room. We need a building more than you who live in the pure air and bright sunshine can know. While it seems I cannot regain my usual strength, I can do a little of the business, and the work goes on."

1047 West Madison Street: Mary Everhart held the first service here on Thanksgiving 1927; it was reopened following renovation on Thanksgiving 1987.

Yet she knew her own antidote: "This is from real life...and my moral is plain. When your hearts are weary and the way seems rough and hard, go and find other hearts more full of care than your own and you will soon forget all of your own troubles in trying to comfort others; you will find that 'It is more blessed to give than to receive.' (Acts 20:35)"

Her energy was renewed and her passions fueled especially by injustices to women and children. She was dismayed that, by 1897, "there are only thirteen police stations in Chicago where women can be taken, and 31,945 women and children were under matrons' care (in them) in one year." She was outraged at finding a child dying from injuries that his father had inflicted in a drunken rage: "He lived in a Christian land, in a country that takes great care to pass laws to protect sheep and diligently legislate over its game. Would that children were as precious as brutes and birds!"

Whatever her own circumstances, Mary always found time to take Sunday School children to the park. When she was trying to raise $20 thousand and struggling to pay the rent, she found space in her newspaper to thank children who had sent her pennies: "Many times when the burden seemed too heavy to carry, some token of your interest, love, and sacrifice has put new courage in our hearts and new strength in our bodies."

She was superintendent of the mission for thirty-five years. The physical needs of the indigent, an ever-present concern, took much of Mary's time and energy, but she saw her primary task as nurturing the souls of those in despair. During her tenure, religious conversions averaged one a day.

Katie V. Hall, superintendent from 1939 to 1952

Mary Everhart died in 1928. Fortunately, a firm cadre of dedicated colleagues—some of whom had first come to the mission back in the 1890s, like Katie V. Hall—had developed to carry on the work. Carry on they did, much as before. They began a school for training urban missionaries, where teachers who were mostly pastors donating their time without pay provided study and practical experience. But the mission's primary goal, religious guidance and feeding, clothing, and loving the poor in the area west of Chicago's Loop, stayed in the forefront.

Mary Everhart's vision for training youth for urban ministry has become today's Wesleyan Urban Coalition, with thirteen participating colleges.

Wars, depressions, and unrest have come and gone, as have social, political, and theological theories about poverty's causes and cures, but the Olive Branch remains Chicago's oldest continuously running mission. For more than a century, its workers have carried on, perhaps never having heard Mary Everhart's dictum, but sharing it nonetheless: "A religion that doesn't cost anything is not the kind the good Samaritan had."

Olive Branch Mission Today

Forty-five garments given out, with twelve baskets of apples, three of onions, one and a half of dried apples, three pints of fruit, in addition to cabbages, quilts, lunches and lodgings.

—*The Olive Branch newspaper, 1904*

Harpo Studios, Oprah Winfrey's production studio, one block north of the Olive Branch

Today, a full-time staff of thirty-six oversees activities at the Olive Branch Mission administrative offices, two neighborhood centers, and four overnight shelters. Over a thousand volunteers also contribute their skills and services every year.

The staff serves six hundred meals a day, distributes donated clothing to 7,800 people a year, and coordinates a range of services from a residential rehabilitation program to overnight winter shelters with two hundred beds.

The Neighborhood Center serves up to one hundred people who need a stable daytime place to get their lives back together. Facilities include showers, clothing, phones, storage, mail, spiritual guidance, and a men's emergency overnight shelter. The center's services include weekly visits from Social Security, Veterans Administration, and Legal Aid for the Homeless counselors; literacy and high school equivalency classes; enrichment sessions in music, art, drama, gardening, physical fitness, and black history; evaluation, referral, and counseling from a social services staff; and daily Alcoholics Anonymous and Cocaine Anonymous sessions.

The Olive Branch also provides apartments for eight men who are motivated to return to independent living through the Intentional Neighbors Program. Space for a women's overnight emergency shelter was acquired in 1990, and it contains apartments for six women in the Intentional Neighbors Program. Overnight shelter is also available at two other Chicago locations that the Olive Branch manages.

Staff and volunteers still write and print *The Olive Branch* newspaper, which is now mailed to sixty thousand donors and friends all over the world. It's been published steadily (although sometimes sporadically) for over a hundred years.

They operate out of crowded quarters in a building on a street that was once the heart of Chicago's "skid row" and is now undergoing "gentrification." Harpo Studios, Oprah Winfrey's renovated 100,000-square-foot, twenty-million-dollar, state-of-the-art production studio fills an entire block one block north of the Olive Branch. Also, the new WCFC-TV 38 and a major construction company's headquarters have moved within blocks, attracting small business and the conversion of warehouses into residential lofts.

Some new neighbors have been very gracious: Oprah Winfrey sends regular donations; a food stylist sends over food after he's photographed it; the employees and the president of Jahn Ollier Printing offer volunteer service; TV 38 had a special drive and donated a thousand blankets; and other busi-

Presidential Towers, a subsidized, 2,346-unit, luxury high rise just six blocks from the Olive Branch and the object of protests by Chicago advocates for the homeless

nesses have sent money.

However, the rapidly changing neighborhood is a mixed blessing. Presidential Towers, a subsidized, 2,346-unit, luxury high rise just six blocks from the Olive Branch has been the object of protests by Chicago advocates for the homeless. It devoured 1,700 low-income housing units and eight small missions, but replaced none of these. In spite of federal subsidies, the project has been exempted from the requirement that 20 percent of its total units be made available for low-income renters. Instead, it used $114 million in low-income housing money for this upper-income development. Presidential Towers defaulted on its federally insured mortgage in March 1991. Housing and Urban Development paid off its $163 million note, the largest default in HUD's history. Developers subsequently are seeking $180 million in tax-exempt bonds from the Illinois Development and Finance Authority to bail them out. Local business groups have an increasing tendency to fight the location of social services in this area. Nearby businesses have stopped two other emergency service programs.

In this area, the Olive Branch Mission tries to create a corridor of caring, where social agencies do everything possible to appropriately perform their services. It supports its neighbors by discouraging the Olive Branch clients from standing in front of their businesses. It belongs to Mayor Daley's "Adopt-a-Street" program to keep West Madison Street clean, and it keeps its own facility attractive and well lit.

| *Funding*

The needs of homeless people seem to grow faster than the cash flow. More money is coming in—about $1.9 million in 1991 against $1.6 million the previous year—but basic service costs are increasing as the homeless population grows. The 1986 budget was only $207,000.

Long-term plans are for minimal expansion on West Madison Street and continued movement to satellite locations throughout the city, especially to church buildings and to other underutilized facilities that may not need to be purchased.

Roughly 71 percent of today's operating expenses come from private funding: individuals, churches, and foundations. Another 18 percent comes from government, primarily the City of Chicago. About 3 percent is earned from a variety of projects.

The City of Chicago Department of Human Services considers the Olive Branch Mission one of the city's premier service providers and frequently asks it to pick up new programs. Mayor Daley has visited, and his office has made a greatly appreciated major contribution.

The Olive Branch Mission has a historical connection with the Free Methodist Church of North America (the original 1876 sewing class was held in a Free Methodist Church), but gets no direct funding from them. About three-fifths of the board of directors are from that denomination, but there are no denominational requirements for staff.

Today's Clients and Staff

The staff today

A few years ago, women made up only about 1 percent of the Olive Branch clients. Now they represent about 15 percent. The age is decreasing rapidly, too. In 1986, the average would have been a man in his fifties. Today, it's in the low thirties.

Increasing problems in the public schools have thrown more young people out onto the streets. The prevalence of drugs has also lowered the ages, since younger people are affected more. The mission works closely with local detoxification programs and with agencies providing residential programs and intensive outpatient treatment. Active addicts can't become part of the Olive Branch residential program. They must first successfully complete a twenty-eight-day treatment program, and then they're under supervision of the staff's addictions counselor. Additional outpatient treatment is also sometimes required.

Most of the women clients have some kind of mental illness. Maria, for instance, has been coming for over four years. She's just recently become willing to take her medication for paranoid schizophrenia. Within weeks of taking the medication, staff members were able to get her housed and living productively.

Workers are heartened to see progress in clients such as Maria. Most people who come in off the street can't become part of the residential program, but 60 percent of those who participate in it for four months or longer go on to independent living, about twenty people a year. That's small to those who focus on numbers and programs rather than on work with individuals, but it's monumental to the twenty people whose lives have become productive.

Volunteers, who instinctively focus on individuals, find they make a difference: two retired principals do GED tutoring; an eighty-year-old woman stops to encourage recovering alcoholics; and a woman asks about the lives of some clients for this book project—and really listens. The two volunteers who have each given over thirty years of service have affected thousands of lives.

The homeless say they're amazed by these volunteers who leave their homes and come here just to talk to them. Those who get off the streets claim that being treated like a person again—and then feeling like one—was the first step in getting their lives back together.

Volunteers—and staff—tend to be spiritually motivated workers. Christians hear "Inasmuch as ye have done it unto one of the least of these, my brethren, ye have done it unto me" (Matt. 25:40). Jewish congregations have rallied to supply and cook entire meals for four hundred. Some simply say their faith calls them to serve and believe that their work will bear fruit in ways they may never know.

What Can One Person Do?

The magnitude of the homeless problem today is so overwhelming that good people are becoming desensitized. Nationally syndicated columnists are writing about—and sharing—anger and hopelessness that many Americans feel toward a problem that worsens each year.

How can one person alleviate this suffering? Perhaps the first step is to move from despair over "the problems of homelessness" to being able to see a homeless individual. Here are other suggestions offered by the Olive Branch staff and volunteers:

- Don't avoid looking a homeless person in the eye. Try saying "good morning."
- Consider volunteering. The skills of average people—whether working for or relating to the indigent—can really make a difference. A volunteer serving a homeless person in any way, while treating her as an individual, begins the process.
- If a group home for formerly homeless people is moving into your neighborhood, ask yourself, "Am I going to picket or am I going to get involved to make it work?"
- Give to literacy or life skills programs, or battered women's shelters.

Finally, the Olive Branch Mission experience suggests that progress requires a shift in the way most Americans think. It requires moving away from big government "solutions," abandoning the fear that "if someone else gets money or power, it takes it away from me," paying the price of long-term relational programs rather than being satisfied with emergency aid, and viewing soup kitchens as necessary in the way that hospital emergency rooms are—to keep people alive while we figure out what's wrong.

It's an extraordinary task, and these are difficult times. But the Olive Branch Mission has a long history of facing tough times, with the help of many caring friends. The staff remains optimistic that Americans still care, that new friends will appear and offer to help, and that they will continue to provide hope and change lives.

The Photographers: Sharon Smith and Wally Wright

The photographers: Sharon Smith and Wally Wright

Our first encounter with the Olive Branch Mission was in 1989 when Carol DeChant asked us to create a photo exhibit honoring the 115th anniversary of the mission.

When we started making documentary photographs in the mission dining room we felt intrusive and unwelcome. People using a soup kitchen usually don't like to be photographed. It seemed to make sense to sit down and get to know people one-to-one. After a number of visits to the mission, we began to feel accepted and the concept of our project changed. We would make individual portraits.

The first series with the gray backdrop was made in a room they called the "library." When the door was open, people wandered in and out and, when the door was shut, others banged on it and demanded to have their picture taken.

We used a 35-millimeter hand-held camera and two strobe lights. We bounced light into a large umbrella and kept the light source very close to the subjects. The soft and flattering light and the simple backdrop took them out of the clutter of the urban landscape and made them appear approachable.

The people were wonderful; they were kind of in awe of the big light and basked in the attention. They opened up, told us stories, philosophies, and even poems. We listened, watched, and waited for the moment.

While photographing, we worked naturally together, one with the camera, the other adjusting the light and keeping the subject engaged. Then we switched roles. This somehow kept us fresh.

A grant from the City of Chicago and some generous help from Gamma Photo Labs made a second group of portraits possible.

We decided to challenge ourselves by working with a square format camera and cropping and composing in the viewfinder. A white backdrop eliminated any editorial manipulation of light on the background.

This time we set up in the Olive Branch conference room—two doors down and three flights up. Though the space wasn't as large—we usually photographed with our backs up against the wall—it allowed us total privacy with one person at a time.

We were ready for the stories now and wanted to include them with the photographs.

The stories were compelling:

"I'm forty-nine years old and have been on drugs since I was fourteen. The pressure is strong when everyone in your neighborhood is into drugs."

A guy, just a kid, says, "My uncle dropped me off and drove away."

Tom is a former insurance underwriter who lived off his savings after the company he worked for folded. The savings are gone now and he's still looking for work and standing in a soup line. "I can't wait to lead a normal life, like I used to."

"I don't look homeless, do I?" Kareem says. He was working on an "oiler" from South Africa when he decided to jump ship in San Francisco. "They say the United States is full of golden opportunity, right? I mean, I don't see it."

And finally, an uplifting one: "I'm on a roll!" Clifton said. He just got a job and an apartment. "Everyone said, 'You can't do it, you can't do it, you can't do it,' and I was, like, 'I can do it. I can do it!'"

We look at street people with a different eye now, and always will. We started out by giving our energies to the project and now we're the ones who have received. Our experience at the Olive Branch Mission has enriched our lives.

We are grateful to have been involved in the lives of these people. We hope our photographs encourage you to get involved, too.

The Photos

LOVE AT THE OLIVE BRANCH

VOLUNTEERS AND GUESTS

GEORGE

Sixty-four-year-old George was eating at the Olive Branch for the first time. When asked where he was staying that night, he replied, "I don't know. I've never been in this predicament before." He was robbed of $525 when he was looking for an apartment. They broke his glasses, but he didn't get hurt because, he said, "I have a tough head." George, who is deaf in one ear, served with General MacArthur in Korea at Yellow River.

JOSEPH

Joseph, 30, said he had a nervous breakdown in high school and went to an institution, which was "helpful in some ways, but also scared me"—he didn't like the side effects of the drugs they tried on him. He was spending half of his monthly government check on a transit pass, traveling for hours seeing the city and visiting museums on free days. "Sometimes in the winter I ride the trains to keep warm."

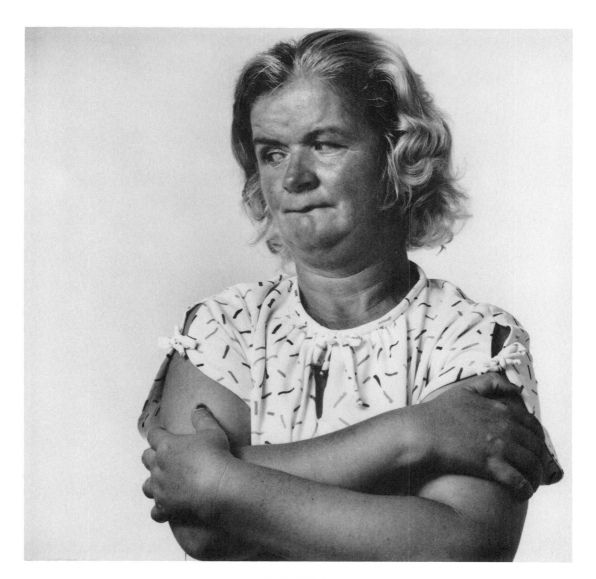

PATRICIA

Her ex-boyfriend got into trouble with the law, leaving her homeless and alone for more than a year. "I've had a boyfriend now for about a year. He's in a job-training program, and we plan to get a place soon, before winter comes."

FRANK

"People tell me I look like Lou Rawls or Chubby Checker," Frank claimed. He and a friend once went through $80,000 of cocaine in five days. He thought of committing suicide when both the police and gangsters were after him. He went cold turkey in prison, but was back on drugs a year after he got out. When he was photographed, he'd been clean for a year and five months and worked as a security guard at the Olive Branch. "The program here is hard, but that's what I needed."

EVA

Eva, a seventy-words-per-minute typist, was laid off from her clerical job at police headquarters because of her depression. At the age of 42, she was worried about getting another job, losing weight, and being homeless. "I don't want to live at the projects. There are too many drugs, too much violence there."

ANNETTE

"Things are coming my way!" Annette reported. She hadn't done drugs for three months "and I feel great about it," she said. She was waiting for an apartment and doing volunteer work each day "to keep occupied." Annette believed that "with the Lord's help and that of the Olive Branch" things would work out for her and her children, who are 12, 8, and 1 years old.

SYLVESTER

Sylvester, who described himself as "outrageous," had been on the street for three days when he was photographed, "trying to get a bus ticket back to Jackson, Mississippi."

STACI AND STEVE

They moved to Chicago from San Antonio when Steve was promised a construction job. After arriving, they learned that the job didn't exist. "I'm going for another job tomorrow. I'll do anything for work because the baby is coming," Steve said. They were married just two hours before this photo was taken. They took a boat ride for their honeymoon, came to the Olive Branch for a meal, and went to sleep in separate parts of a nearby mission.

JAMES

James, 42, had been coming to the Olive Branch for two or three months since he got out of the hospital. "I checked myself in for drinking too much. I've tried AA (Alcoholics Anonymous) but I think it is up to my willpower to quit." He'd been in New Orleans, but returned to Chicago because his mother was sick. "A woman I met in northern Michigan wants me to do some modeling."

CASEY

Casey became a cook at the Olive Branch. He said he liked to write poetry and watch TV and hoped "to sail, horseback ride, and enroll in a cooking school."

JOVAN

"I've been coming to the Olive Branch for a week. I'm just visiting—I'm going back to San Diego tomorrow." Jovan said he exercised daily and slept on the beach. He was a *Playgirl* model in 1984. He graduated from modeling school ten years ago and wanted to pursue an acting career. "I used to study psychology and broadcasting, but quit school. I thought it was better to develop my looks—my body—because that's what really counts."

JAMES

James went to Cuba when he was 17 "and got involved in things to do with the revolution." He'd been in and out of prison since then and called himself a "a sinner, recovering from my past." He said he had "a calling" and told us about "a miracle one morning when a sweet fragrance filled the whole room. There was no more fear. The sun came through the window and left a scar on my arm. I looked in the mirror and my face was red, like a sunburn. I found out later that when in glory Moses' face was red."

ED

This was Ed's first time at the Olive Branch. He'd just been released from the hospital, but had to go back to have his broken jaw set. He'd been mugged and robbed while cashing his welfare check and had no money to fill his prescription or even to phone his mother. He had worked telemarketing and painting and wanted to find a job. Ed didn't want a copy of this picture because he didn't want to remember this time in his life and the pain he was in. "I have some pictures from when I was happier."

CLIFTON

Clifton had just found a job and an apartment. "I'm on a roll. Everyone said, 'You can't do it, you can't do it, you can't do it,' and I was, like, 'I can do it. I can do it!'"

PETRO

"I'm a vagabond," Petro said. "I speak six languages. I used to Cossack dance in Germany, and I play piano and accordion." He wanted to move to Colorado to get his band started again.

JANE

Jane, 65, called herself "a bag lady" and laughed. She described herself as a great-grandmother who once owned three resale stores. She'd had a stroke, resulting in a memory loss, trouble swallowing, and paralysis of her right side. Although she said "I still have trouble with stairs," she was happy with her recovery.

FREDA

Before she was fired, Freda hoped to get her scar from a car accident fixed with the insurance from her job. She said she was illegally locked out of her apartment when her landlord found out she had lost her job. She was sleeping at a shelter and looking for a job every day.

ERIC

"Crossfire, I guess—wrong place at the wrong time. Ain't been right since," Eric said about being shot last year, which almost paralyzed him. Homeless people "have problems inside. They need to talk to someone, do something instead of walking around all day."

TONY

When asked what he wanted to say with his picture, Tony, 38, said, "May life be sweet and livable always."

CHARLES

"People sell their stamps, rob people, just to get the high. A lot of people think life's a joke—the people snorting this China White—there's no excuse. They're selling crack right now in the parking lot across the street. You can't go anywhere to get away from the drugs. The homeless problem will never be solved. You people are making it too easy. People know where they can get a free breakfast, lunch, and where to go for dinner and to sleep."

ARCHIE

Archie, 42, said he was a truck driver for twenty years, but lost his job after several moving violations. When this photo was shot, he had been on the street a week and said, "I didn't know anything about this kind of life." Archie knew things would get better: "Depressed—you can have it. I feel sorry for people who are depressed. When I get back on my feet, I'm going to buy a carton of cigarettes and pass them out to all the guys down here."

RUSTY

Rusty, 62, had been coming to the Olive Branch for ten years and was "very grateful for it." He washed dishes part-time and looked in the trash for aluminum cans to sell. He read National Geographic and loved to visit the Art Institute.

CHRIS

When asked his name, Chris said "shy."

HENRY

"I made some state trooper captain." Henry, 27, had spent four years in a federal penitentiary for running guns. "An old man in prison summed me up real well. I'm the type of guy who gets high on adventure, but I'm getting real tired of it. I just want a normal life, like everyone else. I think I'd like it. I'm trying so hard to stay on the 'straight and narrow.' I know I can get a kilo of coke on credit. Part of me says I'm a knucklehead for not doing it; part of me wants to find a good job, watch my kid grow up, and go fishing."

DARRELL AND CALVIN

Good friends Darrell (left) and Calvin wanted to have their photo made together. Calvin had never been married. Darrell was divorced, "mainly 'cause of the alcohol. I've been through four drug and alcohol rehabs. If you want to quit, you can do it yourself."

MOHAN

Mohan said he was working on an international language to present to the Secretary General of the United Nations. "I learned Chinese at the Defense Language Institute in California and was a translator for the Indian Army during their war with China. I also speak Russian."

REGINALD

At 33, Reginald said he felt "unworthy that I wasted my life just spinning my wheels. Just say *no* 'cause *yes* means you don't have a life. I've been off six months and it's like being reborn. I'm going to recover, go back to college, and get a degree in marketing—guaranteed."

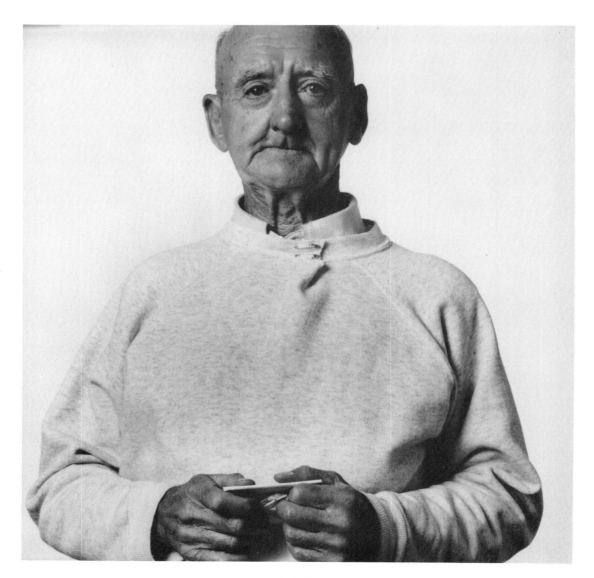

FRANK

Frank, 72, had been coming to the Olive Branch every day, "except when I was in the hospital this summer because of the heat." He stood in the food line, reading a James Bond novel.

JACQUELINE

Jacqueline was taken to a hospital a few days after this photo was taken and no one saw her at the Olive Branch again.

GLENN

Glenn had been eating at the Olive Branch every day and counseling people on drug and alcohol rehabilitation. He wanted to quote Matthew 25:35: "For I was hungry and you gave me something to eat, I was thirsty and you gave me something to drink, I was a stranger and you invited me in; I needed clothes and you clothed me."

DWAYNE

When asked what he did that day, Dwayne said, "Worked."
Doing what? "I went up to people and asked them for money."

HUGH

"I have no family, no relatives. It's just me, myself, and I," said Hugh, 47.

DARWIN

Darwin described himself as a "wild and crazy guy." No more, no less.

CLIFFORD

Clifford, 22, grew up in foster homes and hadn't seen his mother since he was four. "Family isn't something I know, so I don't miss it."

SCOTT

SHAWN

Shawn, 20, remembered celebrating his eighteenth birthday at another mission because his mother had died and his sister couldn't handle him.

JUAN

"All I want is a job in my field—or any job." Juan handed out a neatly typed resume listing a constant employment history since winning the Purple Heart in Vietnam in 1974 and up until a few months before this photograph was taken. He had been a welder, a metal fabricator, a landscaper, a maintenance man, a security guard, and an operator of acetylene torches, forklifts, drill press-es, and Class C vehicles. He practiced martial arts, worked out, and said his physique was "not bad for a 38-year-old man."

RODNEY

BABY

KAT

ANTHONY

Anthony came to the Olive Branch one night confused, depressed, crying, and ready "to give myself over to the Lord." Later he brought a box of sandwiches to the mission from his employer to celebrate that he was working and engaged to be married.

DON

Don's picture was in *Newsweek* with an article on acupuncture treatment for alcoholism, but he relapsed and no one saw him at the Olive Branch after this photo was taken.

MOLLY

RENEE

A "bundle of joy," according to the Olive Branch staff, when she was not high or coming down from a high. They called her "a cocaine tragedy."

DEWEY

A musician, dancer, and harmonica player, his music was jazz, blues, and gospel.

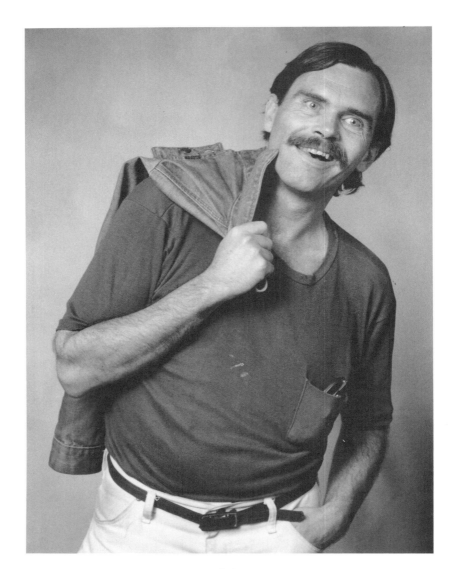

J. R.

JEFF

Jeff, an amputee with a wooden leg, was described by the Olive Branch staff as "cheerful, upbeat—infectiously so—90 percent of the time—but watch out for the other 10 percent!" He had moved into an apartment when the photo was taken.

EVE

One of the first two women in the Olive Branch's residential program, Eve eventually moved out to take a room with a friend in Greektown. During her first year out, she dropped by to keep in touch with the staff and was "always cheerful."

CURTIS

A "success story," Curtis was hired doing maintenance at the Olive Branch and was "doing great," according to staff members.

CHARLES

Charles used to sleep at O'Hare Airport. Travelers and Immigrants Aid gave him food vouchers, but when a restaurant's manager complained that he was "sick of you homeless people coming here," Charles got up and left his food. He has been a volunteer and an employee of the Chicago Coalition for the Homeless. Charles founded and, when this photo was taken, was serving as a volunteer director for HOME (Homeless On the Move for Equality). "Homeless people need to have faith in themselves and *believe* that there *is* hope!"

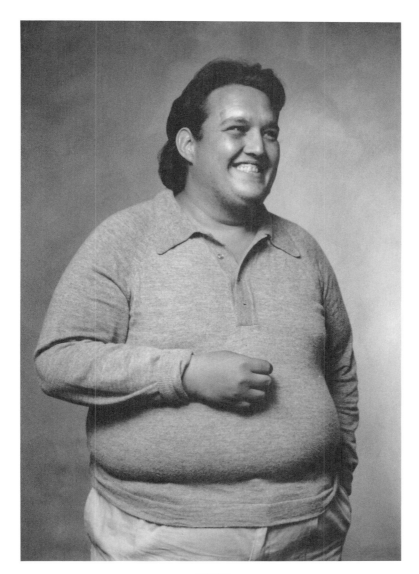

BEAR

MATTIE

Everyone called this 83-year-old woman "Mama." Mattie had her own apartment but not enough money for food, so she came to the Olive Branch almost every Saturday. Her button, "A volunteer is a friend for all seasons," described her well: a Red Cross volunteer for 44 years, a life member of the NAACP, a member of the Chicago Bible Society for 26 years and the Animal Welfare League for 36 years, serving "six terms as president of the oldest club in the district."

THEODORE

ERNESTINE

Ernestine, who was in a day program at the Olive Branch, said she didn't "trust preachers—too much inconsistency," but "I just love to have new friends."

BROWN

JOEY AND ANGIE

Joey and Angie, a married couple, were at the Olive Branch for only two evening meals.

RON

An occasional visitor, Ron said he would quit drinking "some-time" and meanwhile kept in touch with his family "peripherally."

NICKOLOS

MELVIN

BENNIE

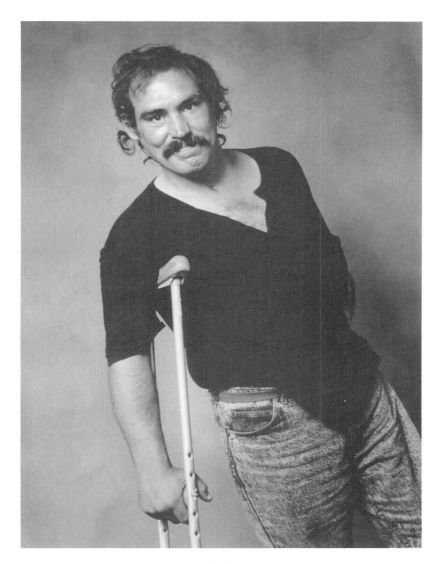

AL

A staff member had just found Al housing and he had been far-ing better than at any time during the fifteen years he'd been coming to the Olive Branch. Ten years before, he'd fallen in front of a car when he was drinking and a hit-and-run driver left him disabled.

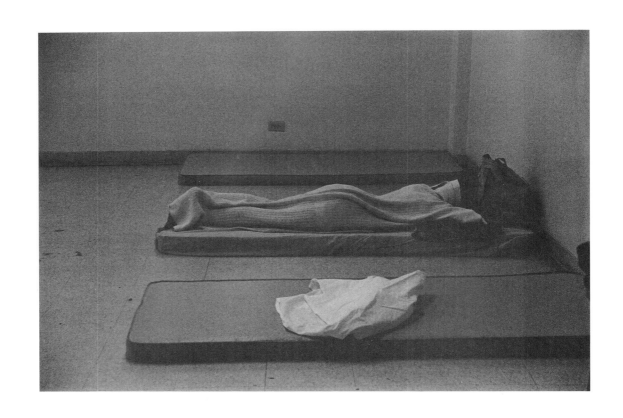

OVERNIGHT IN THE WOMEN'S SHELTER

Sources

Asbury, Herbert. *Gem of the Prairie: An Informal History of the Chicago Underworld*. New York: Alfred A. Knopf, Inc., 1940.

Duis, Perry R. *The Saloon: Public Drinking in Chicago and Boston 1880–1920*. Urbana and Chicago: University of Illinois Press, 1983.

Kogan, Herman, and Lloyd Wendt. *Chicago: A Pictorial History*. New York: E. P. Dutton & Company, 1958.

Lait, Jack, and Lee Mortimer. *Chicago Confidential*. New York: Crown Publishers, 1950.

McCausland, Clare L. *Children of Circumstance*. Chicago: R. R. Donnelly & Sons Company, 1976.

The Olive Branch newspaper. Chicago: various editions.

Stead, William T. *If Christ Came to Chicago*. Evanston: Chicago Historical Bookworks, 1894; reprint 1990.

Taylor, Mrs. Ethel. *The Olive Branch Mission: Past-Present-Future*. 1876–1970 commemorative pamphlet.

Wade, Louise C. *Graham Taylor: Pioneer For Social Justice 1851–1938*. Chicago and London: The University of Chicago Press, 1964.

Woodworth, Ralph. *Light in a Dark Place: The Story of Chicago's Oldest Rescue Mission*. Winona Lake, Indiana: Light and Life Press, 1978.

The Vice Commission of Chicago. *The Social Evil in Chicago*. Chicago: Gunthrop-Warren Printing Company, 1911.

About the Author

Jack Dierks is a native Chicagoan. Jack is a graduate of Beloit College and received an M.S. from the Medill School of Journalism at Northwestern University. He was a newspaper editor in the U.S. Navy. A former public relations consultant and magazine editor, Jack was also a partner in the Porter, Gould & Dierks literary agency for twelve years. He is the author of A Leap to Arms (Lippincott, 1970) and coauthor of The Writer's Manual (ETC Publications, 1977) and contributes magazine articles and book reviews to several publications.